ARRESTED DEVELOPMENT

A Journey to Discovering Identity and

Purpose

TENISHIA B. LESTER

First edition

ISBN: 978-0-578-52982-0

This book was prepared for publication by

DH Book Consulting & Publishing, P.O. Box 3235 McDonough, GA 30253
www.dhbooksandpublishing.com

Cover Design by Shan Mark

DEDICATION

I dedicate this book to my parents, son and grandson.

Table of Contents

FOREWORD

By Dr. Kenneth R. Fleming

This book describes an exciting journey that is difficult, if not impossible, for most to share. A destroyer of life is he who lies in wait to kill, steal, and destroy. Yet Tenisha is an overcomer by the blood of the Lamb, Jesus the Christ, and his anointing, and the word of her testimony Revelations12:11a.

The love of life is a gift that can only be unconditionally given by God. His love prevails. As Tenishia reveals the times of struggle and challenge, you will not hear defeat in this story. While everyone has a story, I challenge you to listen as you read and hear the heart of the matter.

But the LORD said to Samuel, "Do not look at his appearance or at the height of his stature, because I have rejected him; for God sees not as man sees, for man looks at the outward appearance, but the LORD looks at the heart." 1 Samuel 16:7

The lifetime in our flesh is many times remembered and measured by events and life-altering incidents. Too many times we carelessly create incidents and take no thought of the influence that caused others to stumble or remain stuck. There are in this writing, culprits who have been identified but unnamed and forgiven for their indiscretions and transgressions this can only be accomplished in and through the love of God delivered personally by his Son Jesus Christ, and sustained by Holy Spirit as the true comforter and completion of the Triune Godhead.

The love demonstrated in this reflection is from the heart, so we pay attention to the heart message. I intentionally call this book a reflection because the story is far from over. Stay tuned for book two, the continuation of God's daughter. The love of God is continuous and does not come back void, empty, or useless.

To all readers, beware of your hidden things as revelation will come and is drawn from God. This written word should not inspire you to attack your offenders, alternatively, let it draw you closer to God. Let it saturate your inner being and eliminate unforgiveness, guilt, shame or any other feeling or habits. The enemy has leached upon you a multitude of junk to draw all the life from you, even if it is a slow fade that unwittingly separates your destiny from you.

A favorite poem of my youth has directed me to:

...fall still fighting; don't give up whate'er you do... (Guest).

Scripture tells me to "look to the hills, because it is where may help resides. That help is Jesus. Psalms 121:1

Blessings, my loved one. You will always lovingly be my "Squirt".

- Pastor Kenneth R. Fleming, Ed.D.

ACKNOWLEDGEMENT

To my parents, son and grandson, I have only wanted to be the best me that I could be, and I am finally realizing just who that is. Thank you for loving me during my brokenness. I love you.

To my accountability partners, thank you for calling me out, pushing me and praying for me. You know who you are and what you mean to me. I love you.

To those that have contributed to the finished project Write With Me/Beyond the Book Media, DH Book Consulting & Publishing, Vision2Life Publishing Company (Graphics) Thank you very much for walking me through the process.

Special Shout goes out to my uncle Pastor, Dr. Kenneth R. Fleming, Ed.D. for being willing to contribute by writing the foreword. I truly appreciate you for that, I was nervous to ask but Holy Spirit led me to do so.

Finally, but certainly not least, I want to Thank God for keeping me, leading me, guiding me, forgiving me and loving me. Without Him I know without a shadow of doubt I would not be where I am today. Thank you for your Man/Maidservants in the persons of LaBryant and Phineka Friend who you spoke through to assist me in healing.

It is my sincere prayer that this publication reaches all those that need it the most! Be whole, healed and reconciled to God. Remember "There are levels to this Wholeness thing."

INTRODUCTION

Have you ever wondered why it seems as though situations in your life never really pan out or manifest? Maybe, on the other hand, you have been prosperous, but you just feel as though something is missing and you're not sure what?

Often, the problems, or lack of feeling truly fulfilled in our lives, stem from trauma that occurred at some point in our childhood. This trauma could be anything from rejection, abandonment, fear, unforgiveness, sexual abuse, trust and molestation— to name a few. All these hurts and trauma lead to the root issue of a lost sense of identity.

When you were born, there were two destinies assigned to your life. Heaven spoke a divine, purposeful and positively specific destiny over you. Conversely, hell spoke out against your heavenly destiny so that you would exact the purposes intended to steal, kill and destroy your destiny. Your original God-given and purposed identity was perverted due to the trauma you experienced. Well, it is time to reclaim your identity in Christ! Allow me to remind you of who you are.

Arrested Development

In Genesis 1:26 (AMP) it declares that *God said, "Let Us (Father, Son, Holy Spirit) make man in Our image, according to Our likeness{not physical, but spiritual personality and moral likeness];and let them have complete authority over the fish of the sea, the birds of the air, the cattle, and over the entire earth, and over everything that creeps and crawls on the earth."*

Welcome to the journey to discover for the first time your identity for some, and the journey of rediscovery for others. Buckle your seatbelts. This may be a bumpy, but well worth it ride.

The Lies We Tell Ourselves & Others Speak Over Us (Word Curses)

D ue to trauma, past hurts and pains, we often begin to tell ourselves lies. These are referred to as 'word curses'. Truth be told, they are self-fulfilling prophecies. How, you ask? The truth of the matter is that words have power. The Bible says, *"Death and Life are in the power of the tongue, and those who love it and indulge it will eat its fruit and bear the consequences of their words." Proverbs 18:21(AMP)* Therefore, every negative or positive word that flows from your lips is operating on the principle of sowing and reaping. Nothing gives the enemy more pleasure than for you and I to continuously curse or speak death over our lives. The same principle stands for words that others speak over you or what you speak over others.

What are some of the lies that we tell ourselves? I'll start with a few:

1.   I am unlovable.

2. I will never amount to anything.

3. I will never be successful.

4. I am ugly.

5. I am stupid.

6. People are judging me and think I am unintelligent

7. If they knew the real me, they wouldn't like me. I don't even like myself.

These were some of the lies that I have repeated throughout my life. This is not an exhaustive list! Do your work! In my Iyana Vanzant voice, "Take some time to meditate on the lies that you have told yourself." There is space provided below. Don't forget to include what others may have said to you as well — teachers, family, boyfriends, girlfriends you get the picture.

My Word Curse List

_____

_____

_____

_____

_____

_____

_____

_____

_____

_____

_____

_____

_____

_____

_____

_____

_____

_____

Chapter 1

MY STORY

I would like to begin by posing a question. Are you aware that at the point of any childhood trauma, your emotional/social development is stunted or arrested? Allow me to be the first to confirm or present this information to you. Despite being age 46 at the time of this publication and mature in age, I have become acutely aware that my emotional and social development was arrested approximately at the age of five.

I am the only child of a single mother and the eldest and only biological daughter to my father. For all intents and purposes, I was raised as an only child. On many levels, one would/could refer to me as spoiled, of which I can neither confirm nor deny (shhh...I am). There were portions of my childhood that were good, and others that were not.

I grew up in a country setting, where there was a dirt road behind our house and my grandfather had a large garden. Both of my grandfathers were gardeners. The driveway was long, and I had free reign to walk outside barefoot as I pleased. I played freely and followed my aunt and uncle wherever they went, due to our closeness of age, 11 and 10 years respectively. We were always running through peach orchards (yes, we stole a few), climbing 10-foot fences and doing all the other things that kids do. On my father's side, I tagged along with my two aunts as well, and occasionally my uncle. I was raised in church — Primitive Baptist on one side, and Church of God in Christ (COGIC) on the other side.

Chapter 2

THE SHAME OF IT ALL

My earliest recollection, around 5 years old (I remember not being in kindergarten), this is when it all began. I have a vivid picture in my mind's eye of being at the babysitter's house and being sent upstairs to take a nap. I recall laying down with my stuffed rabbit. It was peachy orange in color, with blue on the inner ear and belly. Her oldest son, who had to have been a teenager or early 20's, came into the room. He started out talking to me and then before I knew it, he began to place his hand in my underwear. I can't fathom what could have gone through my 4 to 5-year-old mind.

As an adult looking back, that seemed to have put a target on my forehead, because he would not be my only sexual abuser as time went on. I can vividly recall four other men doing the same — some of which were family members. There were times where it occurred with family members right in the very next room. The way it always happened, and the places it did, it seemed as if no one ever missed my presence.

I can remember being in the 1st or 2nd grade, when a neighborhood girl, who was the same age as I, introduced me to what I now know is referred to as "sex play." She had two younger sisters and at some point, she "played house" with them on a regular basis. She termed it playing "house" or "mommy and daddy"; most often I was the mommy. This went on until she moved to another town.

Again, I became a target — this time another older female abused me in the same manner. Recently, I recalled trying it at that age with other friends. Let's just be honest here, my sexual desires had been awakened prematurely. It also led to a long life of masturbation starting at a young age. At some point, those memories were shut out of my mind. I can only surmise it was self-preservation.

Let's skip forward a bit to the age of 15 — when I lost my virginity. This is when all the memories began to flood my mind like a broken dam. At this age is when the final incident occurred with one of the original family members that first molested me. This incident went all the way this time, with him penetrating me orally and vaginally. When he touched me as I slept, all the memories came back — I froze. I thought if I just laid there and not move, he would go away. Not so! I remember feeling terrified, shameful and hurt. I was terrified when he ejaculated into me! You see, I was an early bloomer and was fully developed at the age of 9, with a menstrual cycle and all other physical attributes. As I am writing, I am wondering if the sexual abuse could have led to my early menstruation...I digress, but it's a real thought.

I had to endure the thoughts and shame — feeling like it was my fault because I was built like a grown woman. I felt like I should have been able to stop it from happening, but I could not. I felt like maybe on some level I asked for it. I felt like it was my fault. I wondered if I told, who was going to believe me at this age? Will I be blamed for it? Well, my worst fear came true when I did tell. I was called a liar and no further action was taken.

I never repeated the story or memories to anyone else. In short, enduring childhood trauma of sexual abuse lead to low self-esteem, lack of confidence, trust issues, feeling unlovable, unworthy, ugly, insecure, shy, introverted and inferior. All those negative characteristics played out in subsequent relationships. I always felt like I had to perform sexually — whether I wanted to or not. I felt that I was only a piece of meat for men to have and use. Social settings made me very uncomfortable. Truth be told, I still have those moments. It also led to a mistrust of females.

How did all this manifest in adulthood? Well, since you asked, of course all my relationships failed. I was even engaged at one point and considering marriage with another. I knew that I would only be doing it because I was afraid to be alone. Feeling as if that would be my only chance to get married, because who would want me, if they knew the real me? To this date I have never been married. On some levels, I am okay with that because I knew in my heart of hearts, that those relationships would have ended in divorce.

At one point, I recall being curious about being with females sexually (which was short lived). I couldn't rationalize the thought of being in a relationship with a woman in my head. Truthfully, I just wanted to satisfy the craving or curiosity of lesbian fantasy. Remember, my body had been trained to respond to female-on-female sex acts, but I liked men. Although, when I watched pornography, I was always aroused by the lesbian scenes; go figure. I can only rationalize it to say my subconscious mind recognized the objectification in the heterosexual scenes compared to the nurturing in the lesbian scenes, like when I "played house."

When I had a child of my own (a boy), I was very protective of him. I did not allow him to stay with many people and I didn't allow people to visit my house. I had to protect him at all costs because I hadn't been protected. This went on well into his pre-teen years. To date, I have a grandson, and I am just as cautious and protective of him. It kills me when he isn't with my son, because I feel like he is not being properly protected. I have learned to keep him in prayer and allow/trust God to protect him. Am I a control freak? Okay... yes, you noticed. I am glad that your discernment is on point. This too is a trait that resulted from being molested. It has allowed me to seemingly protect myself, while simultaneously damaging myself. I say damage, because trusting people has been a real struggle.

Today, I can happily say that three years ago my life was set on a path beyond my control, which lead me to recognize that I was broken and needed to be glued back together — although I was unsure how to make it happen. Not only did I not know how it would happen, I wasn't too sure if it could really happen for me.

Chapter 3

THE HEALING BEGINS

Alittle over a year later, I stumbled upon a challenge on Facebook called "Pray for your Future Spouse." Keep in mind, I was raised in the church, so faith played a role in my life — whether I actively attended or not (you may or may not be a Christian, but this is still applicable). I decided to take the challenge. Despite all the failed relationships, I still would like to get married. As you can guess, there was a caveat to the challenge, on a voluntary basis, however.

The challenge was the prelude to an online platform of several courses that would help to teach men and women like myself how to be "The One" to another. I figured, with all the failures in my past, I could stand to learn a few things. Little did this sister know, it was a divine setup. I like to say that God has a sense of humor, because He is always setting a sister (me) up!

The courses taught me how broken I was and led me on a path to healing. By the end of 2017, I cut ties with an individual I was intimate with to focus on me for once; to truly take the time needed to heal. I completed the program, The One University (TOU). Shout out to Pastors Jamal and Natasha Miller and the Miller Media Group. This experience sparked a hunger in me for more.

During my early moments in TOU, I remember the Millers always referencing their church, All Nations Worship Assembly in Chicago. I began to follow their Pastor, Apostle Matthew L. Stevenson III, on Facebook. Up until this point, I had never heard of the church or the Pastor. Well one day, I found out that there was a branch of the church in the city of Atlanta.

After a little searching, I found some videos on Facebook. The first video that I watched pierced my soul. Have you ever had questions regarding religion or life, and no one seemed to be able to give language to? That is where I was, but I began receiving answers through this Pastor. I decided that no matter where or how far the distance, I needed to go sit in the same space as this man to see if I felt the same way.

All Nations Worship Assembly of Atlanta (affectionately known as ANWA-ATL) is under the leadership of LaBryant and Phineka Friend. One Sunday in December of 2017, I took the 2-hour drive to see what the real deal was. That woman of God, Pastor Phineka Friend, spoke that day. She was raw, eloquent, and real. I mean straight no-chaser... gut punch real! I cried the entire service. Never in all my life had I ever heard a preacher discuss all aspects of their life without sugar-coating it or dismissing the sexual aspects; nor was there any condemnation for anyone else that had committed the same acts.

There was an altar call and I went up for prayer. To this day, I have no clue who prayed for me because I was a teary-eyed, snot-nosed mess. This moment was a life-altering one, in which I had an encounter with the Holy Spirit like no other encounter in my life. It was on this day that I was baptized in the Holy Spirit with the evidence of speaking in tongues. From that moment, I knew that I had to come back and find a way to get there on a regular basis. That church was home, and I did not care how far the drive was.

The first Sunday of the New Year 2018, I officially made ANWA ATL my home and I have been attending regularly ever since. The teachings are nothing short of amazing and life altering — no matter who brings the word. My Pastors believe in and advocate counseling, of which I appreciate so much. I never heard a pastor tell someone to go to counseling. That is unheard of in the black community.

The final component that has contributed to my healing is a concept of "Tribes", that Pastor LaBryant initiated. Tribes are small groups within the church that are interest and location based. As an introvert, I can wholeheartedly say that I was obedient while at the same time kicking and screaming. I flat out said during our first meeting that I would have nothing to contribute. Fast forward to a year later — they know all my business, hold me accountable, call out my shenanigans, and love me unconditionally. Not only that, I now recommend community to everyone. I am now a leader of a tribe myself — go figure (another set-up). Pastor LaBryant says all the time that "ANWA is a place where you can heal; and heal responsibly." That is truly what ANWA has allowed me to start doing and I continue to do so.

Since TOU, I have attended two other life programs or healing ministries under the Desert Stream Ministries umbrella, Cross Current and Living Waters in conjunction with counseling. I would and do highly recommend both programs to anyone. I wish that everyone could be exposed to these programs. In fact, they are across the country in various states. Check the reference section for more details.

This journey has been rewarding and very challenging. My highest moments are when God gives me revelations about who I am in Him. My lowest and most challenging moment to date came to test my "G", in other words my gangster (no I'm not in a gang). The same family member who molested me when I was 15 decided that he was going to come to our house to visit my grandmother. I found myself having to face those feelings and anxieties that arose in me like a rushing flood: anger, fear, guilt, lack of protection and shame. I have every reason to believe that he knew that I lived there, and it was a deliberate act on his part. He did not come, because I had to muster the strength stand up for myself and demand that he not come.

Initially, when I found out about the visit, he was just supposed to be coming for dinner. At this point it was just before 12 noon the day of. I wrestled with thoughts of leaving the house or not leaving and standing my ground. I had reconciled in my mind, that I would stay and be bold.... go me! But when the call came that he wanted to spend the night, I lost my cool! I put my foot down with my family and demanded that he not come period.

For the first time, I was faced with having to relive and reveal my experiences with her relative to my grandmother — only for her to scream at me and act like I was wrong and at fault. That was a serious blow all over again. One thing I can say, is that God will reveal things to heal them. I garnered two things through that experience. I began to reclaim my power by standing up for myself and my mother redeemed herself — she didn't believe me the first time I told her — by finally standing up for me and acknowledging my truth.

Let me put this out there, this book is not to bash my parents by any means. The facts are the facts. My mother was the person that I told and was not believed by, and my father was unaware until I was in my late twenty's to early thirties. As a parent myself, I can honestly say that now I understand that they did their best. I am guilty of feeling as though they did not do enough to protect me, or they didn't do the things I thought they should have done. I am positive that they have some regrets in some areas. That is natural. I too, have them as a parent. So, for that, I can give them grace and forgiveness, knowing that they did their best. Not only do I forgive them, I actively released them from any perceived offense.

Overall, I turned out well, if I say so myself. I say that to say, forgive those who may have, or you felt as though failed you.

Forgiveness is for you, not for them. However, you must release them from the offense. Being offended is a choice, and I choose not to be offended.

Chapter 4

REVELATIONS

A s I dug into the dark and dusty file cabinet of my mind, with the help of the Holy Spirit to remind me, stories were resurfacing. One night, as I laid in bed praying and giving thanks to God for the divine connections and people that He was placing in my life, I remembered yet another instance of abuse. I recall living in one apartment complex and one of my mother's friends came to stay with us briefly. We lived in a two-bedroom— so she slept in my room on the floor. I am unaware of all the circumstances as to her being there, nor do I know the reasons as to why what I am about to recount happened.

For some reason, I recall there being no doorknob on the inside of my bedroom door. She arose early in the mornings to go to work — or at least it seemed that way to me. If I happened to be awake and she was aware of it, the door would be closed and essentially, I would be locked in my room with no way of getting out. I recall needing to go to the bathroom one time, as this happened on several occasions, and I could not get out of my room. It seemed that no one was home, and I was alone. I cried to be let out of the room so that I could use the bathroom. To no avail. I do not recall the length of time before I was allowed out of the room. At some point, my mother had returned to find me locked in my room.

After a few times, I began to just pretend that I was asleep, so that I didn't get locked in the room. This tactic worked once, but I believe that my mom was home that time. This was during the era of "latchkey kids," of which I was one. I concluded that the girlfriend was supposed to be home with me and called herself protecting me by locking me in my room. Or she was outright evil. Honestly, it could have been a combination of the two. I remember her lying, when I told my mom that she locked me in the room on purpose.

This friend did not stay with us very long. However, it was just long enough to inflict damage and establish me to being known as a liar. As I have previously stated, God will reveal situations to you to bring a level of healing and understanding to your life and situations. I thanked the Lord, for bringing this up to see where in my life, patterns were established of people referring to me as a liar. This had helped to shape my false identity. As an adult, I can see how it would be hard to believe that another seemingly responsible adult would lie on a child. I guess this is where knowing your child is would be advantageous.

This would not be the first or last time in my life that I would be called a liar to further one's own agenda to cover up their wrongdoing. It seems this abuse thing runs deeper than I thought on several different levels. It seemed that no matter what I did on occasion, someone would insist that I was lying. Let's be honest, as an only child, who could I have possibly blamed things on? No, I did not have invisible friends, and my cousins were younger than I.

I learned that no one believes the truth, despite constantly telling me to tell the truth. When I lied, it was more readily accepted as the truth; I tested my theory. I learned that the truth did not matter, and no one believed in me. Truth was a subjective matter, that was only regarded insomuch as it served one's agenda. These experiences taught me a few things: One — when I did lie, I could get away with it, two — people do not really want to know the truth as it is, only as they perceive it to be; three — I detest liars and four — I was always responsible no matter the situation.

I learned, throughout all of this, to have grace, and to extend it to my parents for where I felt as though they failed me. I used to blame them for all the unfortunate occurrences in my life, but then the scales began to fall from my eyes. I could see them more clearly, as I stated before. Do not misunderstand me. Sometimes parents are directly the cause of life situations involving their children, then there are times when they just do the best that they know how in the moment.

Have you considered what growing up was like for your parents? Are you aware of their childhood experiences or lack thereof? Have you considered the generational patterns in your family that might have been passed on to you? Personally, I can say unequivocally that there were generational sin cycles and patterns in operation that led to certain decisions or indecisions by my parents. But I am telling my story, not theirs.

I honestly and wholeheartedly believe that families holding secrets are contributing to the deterioration of the family structure and allows sin cycles to be passed from generation to generation. I know everyone has probably heard the old adage, "What goes on in my house stays in my house," at some point in their life. I heard the adage as a child and I most certainly used it as an adult with my child. It's malarkey! STOP THAT! Those secrets are what has allowed "Uncle

Pookie" to molest 3 generations of girls in the family. No one spoke up or defended the children, and as a result, the cycle continued. If by chance, a child told you and you deemed that child a liar, I have one question: Did you do your due diligence and investigate? Perhaps you are the child that did speak up or you want to speak up. Do it. Tell until someone believes you or is adult enough to investigate.

As I stated previously, I spoke up, but was not believed (that identity as a liar I mentioned). As a result, I never told anyone else. I live with the regret of the decision not to tell anyone else daily. I say regret, because I honestly feel in my heart of hearts, that I was not the only one affected by that family member that molested me. I will probably never know, because again, people believe in family secrets. No one wanted to upset the proverbial apple cart and subsequently, being called a liar did not help anyone else or myself. Speak up. You can be the "plot twist" in your family. Will the buck stop with you?

Chapter 5

THE FACT IS

Take a deep breath with me! Due to my experiences with sexual abuse and molestation, my social and emotional development was arrested, and my identity was stolen. I am not speaking in the worldly context of social security numbers and credit cards. I am speaking spiritually — my God given identity, calling and purpose.

I have come to realize that Satan was shaken in his proverbial boots to his core the moment I took my first breath outside of the womb. Why? Because he had a view of what God had created and purposed me for to bring God's kingdom to Earth. Therefore, Satan had to use people to exact his hellacious plot to kill, steal and destroy me (my destiny, as stated previously) as it says in John 10:10. While he was unsuccessful in physically killing me, he stole my identity and the lack of identity almost destroyed me. What he did not calculate was all the things that God had in my scroll that would lead to me beginning to reclaim my identity and discover my purpose.

Have I always known my purpose? No, I did not, not until 2018, when I finally received instructions on how to ask and listen for God's response. *Matthew 7:7 says "ask and it shall be given..."*, that is what I did. I asked God for an audible voice and He complied. Literally, up until that day, I had spent most of my adult life going back and forth to school trying to find the right major and never achieving the goal of obtaining a degree. Since the day God spoke to me, my school life has been progressing in a positive direction. The enemy still tries to discourage me, and some days he is successful, but God!

So, my journey has been learning to rediscover my identity in Christ. You see, there has always been a void in my life and heart, that I used sex and men to fill. (Remember, I asked if you felt a lack of fulfillment in your life.) The reality was/is that the void I felt, only God could fill. But due to the lack of knowledge of my identity, I remained unfulfilled. I have learned that when you allow God to love you, you begin to love yourself from a pure place, not egotistically. If you cannot truly love yourself properly and gracefully, certainly no one else will. Ask me how I know! The saying is true, "Hurt people, hurt people." I have been hurt and I have hurt people, for which I am truly sorry and have reached out to some to just apologize.

I invite you to spend the next 14 days with me to learn about what God has to say about your identity. This will help to facilitate you beginning to love yourself. Allow God to love you, be whole and reconciled to God as Abba, your Father and you as son/daughter. **NO** this is not a one-shot deal. Do not misunderstand me. We often think and look for quick fixes, but this is not that! Wholeness and healing are an ongoing process. You will never be done. You are not your experiences, but you are most certainly responsible for how you handle them. You alone are responsible for the manner in which you heal from any trauma you experienced. As I stated, you have to be diligent in managing your emotions and healing. Choose today to not allow offense to rule your life. Choose today to make a proactive choice to heal.

Chapter 6

WORK IT OUT!

In this part of the book, we will work together to help you uncover the lies and discover the truth about who you were created to be. The next section you encounter will include the following seven components to get you started:

1. 14 days of topics regarding what God says about you
2. A scripture
3. A question to ponder -QOTD (can be answered in the Reflection)
4. A discussion
5. A prayer starter
6. An affirmation for the day
7. Reflection (write whatever surfaces for you, answer the QOTD)
8. Finally, write letters of reflection to your younger self, parents or abusers.
9. Reflection (write whatever surfaces for you, answer the QOTD)
10. Finally, write letters of reflection to your younger self, parents or abusers.

Enjoy the next 14 days. Allow yourself to feel whatever emotions God reveals to you. He reveals things to bring about healing and restoration. Be present and open. Above all else, be gracious to yourself.

Grace, according to Merriam-Webster, is mercy, pardon, a special favor, a disposition to or an act or instance of kindness, courtesy, or clemency. If God extends mercy and grace to us, why do we find it hard to extend to ourselves? I encourage you to find additional scriptures, quotes, poems and create affirmations for yourself in addition to those provided.

Chapter 7

CHOSEN

Even before he made the world, God loved us and chose us in Christ to be holy and without fault in his eyes. Ephesians 1:4 NLT

Have you ever felt unwanted/unchosen/castaway?

AFFIRMATION: I AM CHOSEN BY GOD; HE CHOOSES ME DAILY AND I CHOSE MYSELF DAILY.

If you have ever felt this way, trust me when I tell you, you are in good company. I probably felt unwanted most of my life. Rejection has an uncanny way of making you feel this way. Whether you were rejected by peers, family or parents, feeling unwanted is the result. I remember being the last to be chosen for kickball in school. NO ONE wants to be that kid, right! Well, your girl was, on occasion. That is just one example that most people can probably relate to, but what about not feeling as loved as a sibling, or not being the favorite child?

In the natural, you may have been unwanted, and there are various reasons, be it an unwanted pregnancy as a result of rape or molestation, rejection of the father/mother while in the womb, adoption, abandonment or a result of postpartum depression. Whatever the case, not to trivialize the situation, the cold fact is that your feeling of being unwanted is a trick of the enemy. Satan wants to keep you in a rejected state of mind. Let me say that again, SATAN WANTS TO KEEP YOU FEELING REJECTED AND UNWANTED!

If Satan can keep you in that mindset, then he has won the battle and is in no danger of you discovering who God has called you to be. God chose you before the foundation and creation of the earth. Yes, God called you, (insert your name here)! Frankly, God chose the vessels that were used to impart life to you also (your mother and father). God knew who they were and their capacity when he chose them also to be the vessels in which to bring forth your being.

Once you can grasp this revelation, you are on the path to discovering who you are in Christ and solidifying your identity. This revelation causes Satan to quake in his boots!

Why, I am glad that you asked. When God chose you, trust and believe, He had/has a plan and purpose for your creation. You were designed with a specific purpose to solve a problem in the earth realm, that ONLY you can fulfill.

PRAYER KICKOFF: Father, help me to rest in the knowledge that you chose me before the creation of the world, according to Ephesians 1:4. Thank you for choosing me and choosing the vessels that brought forth my being. Father forgive me for not choosing myself and rejecting myself as a result of being rejected by others. Today, and all days going forward, I choose me. I declare and decree that I am chosen of God.

REFLECTION:_____

_____

_____

_____

_____

_____

_____

_____

_____

_____

_____

_____

_____

_____

_____

_____

_____

_____

_____

_____

_____

_____

Chapter 8

MASTERPIECE/WORKMANSHIP

EPHESIANS 2:10 For we are His workmanship [His own master work, a work of art], created in Christ Jesus [reborn from above—spiritually transformed, renewed, ready to be used] for good works, which God prepared [for us] beforehand [taking paths which He set], so that we would walk in them [living the good life which He prearranged and made ready for us.]

How would you feel if someone berated your creation, your child, artwork, or project?

AFFIRMATION: God is the potter and I am the clay. I am His masterpiece, a wonderful work of art.

God calls us his masterpiece, He made each of us in His likeness and image! We often talk down to ourselves or allow others to do so. However, when you know better, you do better. So, this is what transpires when you talk down to yourself, you begin to contradict God. Let that digest! Every time you disqualify yourself, ridicule yourself, berate yourself and speak death over yourself, you literally tell God, "You created junk, a worthless piece of nothing." all of which is UNTRUE! Imagine how God feels when we say such things over ourselves... take some time to consider that.

Here is something else to consider: thoughts become thought patterns, thought patterns turn into spoken words and spoken words shape your world. This is how the enemy begins to take up space in our minds. Your mind is what rules your life — whether you thought about it that way or not. Our struggles always begin in the mind.

This took some time for me to grasp, and I still have to remind myself that I am a masterpiece. Counseling can be of great use in the area of changing mindset. It most certainly was a big help for me.

PRAYER KICKOFF: Father, help me to see myself as the masterpiece that you have created me to be. I know that you don't make mistakes. You were intentional about everything you created — and that includes me. I confess and repent that I have viewed myself through faulty lenses. Forgive me. I will no longer accept the opinion of others regarding my identity as anything short of being your masterpiece.

REFLECTION:_____

_____

_____

_____

_____

_____

_____

_____

_____

_____

_____

_____

_____

_____

_____

_____

_____

_____

_____

Chapter 9

FRIEND

John 15:12-16 (NLT) This is my commandment: Love each other in the same way I have loved you. There is no greater love than to lay down one's life for one's friends. You are my friends if you do what I command. I no longer call you slaves, because a master doesn't confide in his slaves. Now you are my friends, since I have told you everything the Father told me. You didn't choose me. I chose you...

How do you treat your friends, what do you require of them?

AFFIRMATION: God calls me friend! I am a friend of God!

The way we treat our friends, speaks directly to our character. Are you a friend of exceptional character? Or are you the shady friend? Sometimes we treat others as we want to be treated. We tell them all our deepest and darkest secrets. Others, we deal with at arm's length. I can recall times when I was a better friend than the friendship I received in return. I believe at some point in life, we all encounter those selfish people, no matter the relationship (platonic or intimate). Often this, as well as childhood trauma, leads to trust issues. Unwittingly, these things can also be how we relate to God.

This may seem like a farfetched concept but trust me when I tell you, it is not. God, like the faithful, "ride or die" (pun unintended) that He is, is just waiting for us to call on Him. He wants to hear our darkest secrets, fears, anxieties, successes and losses. Just as you would cultivate a relationship with someone you just met or a longtime friend, the same concept holds true being a friend of God. As with some friends who know you so well that they know your thoughts and actions, God knows also. Psalms 139:1-4 (NLT) says: *O Lord, you have examined my heart and know everything about me. You know when I sit down or stand up. You know my thoughts even when I'm far away. You see me when I travel and when I rest at home. You know everything I do. You know what I am going to say even before I say it, Lord.*

Who wouldn't want a friend that you can always depend on?

PRAYER KICKOFF: Lord, I admit that I need to learn what it means to be a true friend and accept being your friend. Thank you for being mindful of me that you saw fit to call me friend. Thank you for being willing to share all my secrets, fears, pains, successes and losses.

REFLECTION:_____

_____

_____

_____

_____

_____

_____

_____

_____

_____

_____

_____

_____

_____

_____

_____

_____

_____

_____

_____

_____

_____

_____

_____

Chapter 10

SON/DAUGHTER

2 CORINTHIANS 6:18 (AMP) And I will be a Father to you, and you will be My sons and daughters, says the Lord Almighty.

Have you ever felt like an orphan or wished you had different parents?

AFFIRMATION: I am God's child, a son/daughter of the King.

I remember being upset with my mother as a child and making statements like: "I wish I could have chosen my parents", "I wish so and so was my mom", "God why did I have to be born into this family?" If you're honest, you can probably admit the same. Unfortunately, we cannot choose those that we are related to or the situations in which we were born.

On the flip side, for those of you that may have been abandoned as a child and raised in the foster care system or even adopted by another family, you too were not a mistake. Feelings of being unloved, unwanted, abandoned, rejected, cast aside and downright abused can lead to what is referred to as the "orphan heart." The orphan heart tells us that the situations we endured or are currently in are unchangeable and hopeless. Therefore, we accept them as the norm, albeit contrary to the will of God. These strongholds are a tactic of the enemy to keep you bound and in a belief system that says you are not good enough, you won't be excepted, you will never be blessed or loved.

These are situations that God endured while He walked among men and redeemed us from, through His shed blood on the cross. He totally understands. There was no mistake made by God in using the vessels He chose to bring about our lives. God did not make a mistake or error in creating us. In fact, He was so pleased with His creation that He stepped back and said, "That is good." Have you ever created or completed something, and took a minute to assess your work and had to pat yourself on the back because it was "good?"

PRAYER KICKOFF: Father, your Word says that you adopted us as your own children in Romans 8:15. I confess that I have felt all the emotions consistent with an orphan heart such as anger, rage, jealousy, lack of joy, etc. Teach me how to view you as a loving and faithful Father that will not leave me nor forsake me, but willingly takes me up when my earthly mother or father has forsaken me.

49

REFLECTION:_____

_____

_____

_____

_____

_____

_____

_____

_____

_____

_____

_____

_____

_____

_____

_____

_____

_____

_____

_____

_____

_____

Arrested Development

Chapter 11

HEIR

Romans 8:17 (AMP)And if [we are His] children, [then we are His] heirs also: heirs of God and fellow heirs with Christ [sharing His spiritual blessing and inheritance], if indeed we share in His suffering so that we may also share in His glory.

What does it mean to have an inheritance?

AFFIRMATION: I am a joint heir with Christ.

Merriam-Webster defines an heir as one who receives property from an ancestor; one who is entitled to inherit property; one who receives or is entitled to receive something other than property from a parent or predecessor. Biblically speaking, the property of a father would be split between the sons born to legitimate wives. The eldest son would receive the largest portion in relation to any other sons. In *Galatians 4:7*, it refers to you and I as heirs in receipt of valuable gifts from God. Due to the redemptive work of Christ on the cross, you and I are no longer considered to be "slaves" but sons of God, just as Jesus Christ.

What is meant by "slaves?" When I refer to being a slave, I mean that there is no amount of "works" that we could do to become pleasing, loveable, or worthy in God's sight. In stark contrast to God, people often want you to earn their love or acceptance/affirmation in various ways.

For example, as children, we are affirmed by the grades we make in school, the extra-curricular activities, your position in the family; the list could go on. I can remember trying to "ensure" men loved me by always being available and adhering to their sexual desires, wants and whims despite my own. The truth is there was no amount of pleasing that I could have done to make them love me. There was nothing I could have done to make them stay with me or be faithful.

God says, "not so!" Isn't it refreshing to know that you do not have to do anything to earn His love?

PRAYER KICKOFF: Gracious Father, thank you for loving me just as I am and deeming me enough. Thank you for not

requiring me to earn your love and affection. You willingly give me your love; I just need to be receptive of it. Thank you for

calling me an heir to all the things that you have afforded to Jesus Christ your son.

REFLECTION:_____

_____

_____

_____

_____

_____

_____

_____

_____

_____

_____

_____

_____

_____

_____

Arrested Development

Chapter 12

Adopted

Ephesians 1:5 (AMP) He predestined and lovingly planned for us to be adopted to Himself as [His own] children through Jesus Christ, in accordance with the kind intention and good pleasure of His will--

Do you operate from the heart of an orphan or an adopted child?

AFFIRMATION: I AM A CHILD OF THE KING, THE LORD MOST HIGH. HE IS MY DADDY!

To operate from the heart posture of an orphan, is when you are constantly striving for love, trying to control people and situations, not loving yourself and trying to fit in — to name a few. I operated this way much of my life. I always felt as though I didn't measure up or fit in. If you too feel this way it is a good chance that your heart posture is that of an orphan.

Let's look at this in a practical way. What are some characteristics of those we have seen or encountered (you maybe have grown up in the foster care system) that society labels as orphans? Rejected, abandoned, lost, uncared for, unloved, (you fill in the blanks) _____. These individuals often feel like they do not belong to someone or something.

Truthfully, one can feel all these feelings and belong to a family yet feel as an outsider. This is my story. I never felt as if I fit in. I always felt like the "black sheep," "the odd ball," and "the strange one." These characteristics can often be perpetrated in other relationships as we mature. For instance, that clingy ex-girl/boyfriend that wanted to know your every waking move. God says, in *Psalms 27:10 Although my father and my mother have abandoned me, Yet the Lord will take me up [adopt me as His child].* Therefore, according to the word, God is our father, whether we have a person fulfilling that role or not. God willingly and freely accepts responsibility of us as His children. God has ADOPTED YOU!

PRAYER KICKOFF: My God, I confess and ask you to forgive me for operating from the heart of an orphan. Allow me to feel your love as a willing parent. Free my heart and mind to see you as Daddy God. I no longer want to view you as one who punishes, judges, gets angry or leaves me. You are always willing to be by my side.

REFLECTION:_____

_____

_____

_____

_____

_____

_____

_____

_____

_____

_____

_____

_____

_____

_____

_____

_____

_____

_____

_____

_____

_____

_____

_____

_____

Arrested Development

Chapter 13

COMPLETE/WHOLE

Colossians 2:10-11 (NLT) So you also are complete through our union with Christ, who is the head over every ruler and authority. When you came to Christ, you were "circumcised," but not by a physical procedure. Christ performed a spiritual circumcision- the cutting away of your sinful nature.

Have you been reconciled to Christ from your sinful nature?

AFFIRMATION: I am complete in Christ Jesus!

The Bible speaks of us being born in sin, which is a result of the fall of man. When Adam and Eve sinned in the Garden of Eden, that led to the fall of man and us as descendants being born into sin. It probably seems strange and you may ask, how can you be a sinner as a newborn baby? Well, by the sheer nature of the curse placed on man at the time of Adam's fall.

Thanks be to God; we can now be made clean and whole through Him. In the Old Testament days, one would simply go to the priest with an offering for the atonement of sins and he would present burnt offerings on our behalf to the Lord. This sacrifice was only performed once a year (Leviticus 16:34). When Jesus died, He became the ultimate sacrifice for all our sins, therefore eliminating the need to make atonement once a year. The veil to the entrance of the Holy of Holies was torn and we now have access to God to repent for our own sins, the priest is no longer needed.

So, it is by the confessing and repenting of our sins that allows for us to make atonement to God and for the remission of our sins. We can now boldly approach the Throne of Grace (*Ephesians 3:12 NLT*) through faith and with confidence that God hears us and forgives us. Scripture says that we are new creatures in Christ Jesus. (*Eph 1:7, Heb. 9:14, Col. 1:14)* Have you confessed your sins and asked God to forgive you, so that you may obtain wholeness and become complete in Christ?

PRAYER KICKOFF: Father, I thank you for taking on all of humanity, that I may now come to you boldly to confess my sins and be forgiven. I confess with my mouth and believe in my heart that I am a sinner and that you came to redeem me. I believe that you were born, died and was resurrected for the remission of my sins. I thank you for becoming the ultimate sacrifice so that I may be whole and complete in you.

REFLECTION:_____

_____

_____

_____

_____

_____

_____

_____

_____

_____

_____

_____

_____

_____

_____

_____

_____

_____

_____

_____

_____

_____

_____

_____

Arrested Development

Chapter 14

TREASURE

Deuteronomy 7:6 (AMP) For you are a holy people [set apart] to the Lord your God; the Lord your God has chosen you out of all the peoples on the face of the earth to be a people for His own possession [that is, His very special treasure].

What do you treasure?

AFFIRMATION: I am treasured by God!

When you think about "treasuring" something or someone, that is saying that you hold them in high esteem, or close to your heart. These people are the ones that get special and preferential treatment from you. The relationship can be that of a parent/child, special friend or husband/wife — you get the picture. A treasure can be a special possession, a family heirloom passed from generation to generation; something that is rare or one-of-a-kind.

Well my friend, that is how God your father views you. You are special to God just as you are. No, He is not concerned with your flaws, sins, mistakes, shortcomings, or proclivities; He loves you just as you are. If God is the creator of all things, don't you think that He is aware of all that you are/are not? He is acutely aware, He made you that way. There is nothing that you or I could EVER do that would cause His view of us to be diminished. *Psalms 139:1 says "O Lord, you have examined my heart and know everything about me. Jeremiah 1:5 (NLT) states "I knew you before I formed you in your mother's womb..."* I equate Abba knowing me to myself as a mother knowing things about my son that he is not aware that I know. Yet, there is nothing that my son could do that would diminish my love for him, nor his position in my heart.

The Love of Our heavenly Father, Abba, Daddy God is the same! You are very special to Abba and there is nothing you can do about it!

PRAYER KICKOFF: Abba, help me to know and rest securely in the fact that you call me "Treasure," that I am special to you and there is nothing that I could ever do to change that.

REFLECTION:_____

_____

_____

_____

_____

_____

_____

_____

_____

_____

_____

_____

_____

_____

_____

_____

_____

_____

_____

_____

_____

_____

_____

Chapter 15

Forgiven

Matthew 6:12 (NLT) and forgive us our sins, as we have forgiven those who sin against us.

Do you find it easy or hard to forgive? Do you believe that God has forgiven you?

AFFRMATION: I am forgiven, and I forgive others more readily.

This is a tough and touchy subject. It's safe to say that when someone has done you wrong once, you can usually see your way through to forgive them. Is it hard? Most certainly, but not impossible, right? The situation becomes sticky when you have been done wrong multiple times by the same person. Why is it so difficult?

Conventional wisdom tells us that you should not forgive someone that consistently does you wrong or causes you harm. And we definitely say one of two things: "Fool me once shame on you. Fool me twice shame on me!" or "I can forgive, but I won't forget." Have you ever uttered those words before? I know I have many times. So, let me tell you my previous rationale, then I will tell you the truth.

My previous rationale said that I needed to protect myself from anyone that would intentionally try to wrong me and cause me harm. I felt as though people took me forgiving them as a weakness and that I could be used as a doormat. Well, I would show them; I just would not forgive or forget. Consequently, I held grudges with two hands and both feet. I also had a real tendency to "cut" people out of my life, quickly.

Now, here is the truth of the matter, we are to forgive. I know, easier said than done. Let me explain why. Fact is, the number one reason is because God forgave us of all our sins. He didn't pick and choose what He would or would not forgive us for. We only need to confess, and our sins are forgiven as it says in *1 John 1:9 (NLT) But if we confess our sins to him, he is faithful and just to forgive us our sins and to cleanse us from all wickedness.* Therefore, if God can forgive us, who are we not to forgive others? *Ephesians 4:23 (NLT) Instead, be kind to each other, tenderhearted forgiving one another, just as God through Christ has forgiven you.*

Secondly, while it may feel as though forgiveness is for the other person, truth be told, forgiveness is for you, the offended one. I know, that doesn't seem to make sense. Here is why forgiveness is for you. According to a CBN news report unforgiveness is causing disease processes in our bodies. We are harming ourselves when we refuse to forgive. We harbor anger, bitterness, hatred, anxiety, etc. If you can't seem to work it out on your own, I admonish you to seek a counselor to help you work through it. The lack of forgiveness is the number one thing that takes up space in our minds and creates those negative mindsets. (Johnson, 2015)

Finally, there is no limit on the number of times that we are supposed to forgive. Yes, this is most definitely contrary to what we think, as I previously stated. Check out the parable (lesson) in the bible in Matthew 18: 21-35. Briefly put, God requires us to forgive seventy times seven times (70x7) not 77 times, don't misread or misinterpret. Say it with me, **"That's A LOT."**

You may have noticed that I talked about this topic in more detail. The reason is because this is one of the most crucial areas that I could ever touch on. It carries an abundance of weight in our lives. This was a hard but necessary lesson for me to learn. I pray this saves you the trouble, wasted time, and reflects the importance of forgiveness; not to negate the importance of the other subjects.

PRAYER KICKOFF: Father I confess that I have operated in unforgiveness. Forgive me. I have held onto situations with bitterness, anger, malice, hatred and all other negative feelings. Help me to understand that You forgave me, and that it is essential for me to forgive others, so that when I confess of my sins, you will forgive me.

REFLECTION: Really take the time to reflect on who you have not forgiven and why. Search your heart and see if by chance unforgiveness could be the reason for any sickness.

_____

_____

_____

_____

_____

_____

_____

_____

_____

_____

_____

_____

_____

_____

_____

_____

_____

_____

_____

_____

_____

_____

_____

_____

_____

_____

_____

_____

_____

_____

_____

_____

_____

_____

_____

_____

_____

_____

_____

_____

_____

_____

_____

_____

_____

_____

_____

Chapter 16

BELOVED

Song of Solomon 2:16 (KJV) My beloved is mine and I am His

What does it really mean to be "beloved?"

AFFIRMATION: I am the beloved of God Almighty.

Have you ever been in a romantic relationship and just felt head-over-heels in love with that person? Well, to be the beloved of someone places that person as the object of one's affection. That my friend, is how God the Father views you and me. We are the beloved of God. We are the apples of His eye, as stated in *Psalms 17:8 (KJV)*. *"Keep me as the apple of the eye..."*

I'm sure you can recall a time in your life when you felt the love of another, be it a parent or romantic relationship. I mean, you knew beyond a shadow of doubt that she/he was totally enamored with you, and their faces lit up with adoration when they spoke about or looked at you. What if I told you that you can feel that unconditionally, at all times?

God wants you to know that you are beloved, and He holds you in the highest regard. He takes pride in you, all that you are and are not, all that you are and are becoming. God only always wants the best for you.

Admittedly, I never really felt this way, even though I was raised in the church. Why? How is that even possible? Well, due to all the situations that I endured, it was hard to see how a God that loved me, or was enamored with me, could allow all those situations to occur. It took me going to counseling and other programs that I mentioned earlier, for me to believe.

If you have ever had the same thoughts that I did, here is the answer. Everything, that you have endured and SURVIVED (you are still living so you survived) was not for you/me. Trust me when I tell you that your story is for someone else to overcome, and you to be the living witness that it is POSSIBLE! How do I know? If I had not gone through, you would NOT have this book in your hands in this very moment. Your trials are directly connected to your purpose and calling in life. Remember we discussed your God given purpose, and that you're the solution to a problem on the earth? My dear, God created you for a purpose and again it is tied to your struggles and situations. Take a deep breath!

PRAYER KICKOFF: Lord, I thank you for calling me your beloved, and being the apple of your eye. Help me to feel and see that. Remind me that I am special to you. Help me to see that although you allowed me to go through situations in my life, you never left me. You were there all the time. Help me to see and reveal to me what the purpose was behind all of my struggles. Show me my purpose so that others may be able to succeed in spite of my tests.

REFLECTION:_____

_____

_____

_____

_____

_____

_____

_____

_____

_____

_____

_____

_____

_____

_____

_____

_____

_____

_____

_____

_____

_____

_____

_____

_____

_____

Chapter 17

CAPABLE / QUALIFIED / SIGNIFICANT

Philippians 4:13 (AMP) I can do all things [which He has called me to do] through Him who strengthens and empowers me [to fulfill His purpose- I am self-sufficient in Christ's sufficiency; I am ready for anything and equal to anything through Him who infuses me with inner strength and confident peace.]

Have you ever felt incapable/unqualified/insignificant?

AFFIRMATION: I CAN DO ALL THINGS BECAUSE GOD SAID I CAN. I AM CAPABLE, QUALIFIED AND SIGNIFICANT!

Most often, and I will speak for myself, we feel unqualified/incapable, et cetera, because someone may have said we couldn't do something, that we were stupid, or we told ourselves those lies. That is what happened in my case: I was told I was lazy or couldn't do things by some people in my life. I was also compared to others. This is what we refer to as "word curses" (you should have listed those at the beginning of the book). Due to the word curses, I began to compare myself to others, and I never measured up in my eyes or in the eyes of others. My teeth were too crooked (I sucked my thumb into my 30's). I was too short. I was too dark-skinned. You name it, I probably said it.

Let me tell you that comparison is the killer of purpose. There will always be something or someone to compare yourself to. The real question is: Why do we believe the lies? Allow me to get a little "churchy" for a minute. There is nothing that Satan would and loves more than a people/person that is not operating in their purpose and allowing comparison to stifle and silence their voice. Yes, there are people doing things better than you, who look better than you, all of that. But you are you, and no one can do you better THAN YOU! We all have our place in the world. We all have our roles to play.

Yes, these feelings will creep in from time to time. Truth be told, I have those feelings about writing this book. "I am not an author," I said. "I don't have any degrees. Who will listen to what I have to say? Who will buy this book?" The list could go on....The truth of the matter is this, no one can say what you will say. Nor can anyone say what you do like you. Seems rather elementary, huh? Well, yea it is!

BE YOU — UNEQUIVOCALLY, & UNAPOLOGETICALLY!

PRAYER KICKOFF: Abba, it's hard not to compare myself in a world where comparison is the norm. Your word says *Do not be conformed to this world [any longer with its superficial values and customs] but be transformed and progressively changed... in Romans 12:2.* So Abba I ask that you continue to show me who I am. I cancel all the lies and word curses that I have spoken and have been spoken over me and cast them to the foot of the cross to be covered by the blood of Jesus. Renew and solidify my identity in you, God.

REFLECTION:_____

_____

_____

_____

_____

_____

_____

_____

_____

_____

_____

_____

_____

_____

_____

_____

_____

_____

_____

_____

_____

_____

_____

_____

_____

_____

Arrested Development

Chapter 18

GOD'S TEMPLE

1 Corinthians 3:16 (AMP) Do you not know and understand that you [the church] are the temple of God and that the Spirit of God dwells [permanently] in you [collectively and individually]?

How are you handling God's dwelling place, your body?

AFFIRMATION: MY BODY IS SACRED SPACE!

I am pretty certain that you have heard that your body is a temple. Having said that, we are to treat it as such. It is important what we put in our bodies and how we treat our bodies. If God himself where to knock on your front door, would you allow him into a dirty, rat infested, smelly and dusty house? I would venture to say, that you would not. Therefore, it is the same with our bodily houses, our temples.

Do we always eat right, exercise, monitor what we watch, hear or speak? Probably not. But that does not mean that we shouldn't. I too am guilty of this very thing. I like sweets and ice cream. I can massacre a pint of ice cream while sitting in my bed in front of the television at night. Because I can, does not mean that I should. I do, but I am making a concerted effort to limit the amount that I ingest. Exercising is a horse of a different color. In all seriousness, injuries prevent me from doing what I prefer although I detest the gym. But there are methods that I can explore, like aqua exercises.

The same can be said for what we watch on television, listen to on the radio, activities we participate in (drugs, sex and the like) and read. I personally cannot listen to certain music because I know that it reminds me of particular situations and people. Most of which I don't want to remember, not that they were all bad...But you get my point. I used to read all the romance novels and smut books; now that is not something that I indulge in because like the Bible says, all things are permissible but not beneficial *(1 Corinthians 10:23 & 1 Corinthians 6:12).*

Lastly, while I have indulged in pre-marital sex, I now choose not to until God sends me a covenant relationship (husband). Believe that with me: I will be a married woman, in Jesus name (smile). I said all of that to say, if you are saved, you believe that Christ died for the remission of your sins; if you confess to be a Christian, then God lives on the inside of you. Therefore, there is a manner in which we should treat our bodies. Having said that, you should want to maintain a healthy lifestyle regardless of beliefs.

All I'm saying is know your limitations/proclivities. I won't get "preachy" or "churchy" with this.

PRAYER KICKOFF: Jesus forgive me for not treating my body, your temple, as the sacred dwelling place that it is. Help me to be more cognizant of what I digest. Teach me to be more selective in my choices of sustenance, reading, hearing, activities and viewing material.

REFLECTION:_____

_____

_____

_____

_____

_____

_____

_____

_____

_____

_____

_____

_____

_____

_____

_____

_____

_____

_____

_____

_____

_____

_____

_____

_____

_____

_____

_____

_____

_____

_____

_____

_____

_____

_____

_____

_____

_____

_____

_____

_____

_____

_____

_____

_____

_____

_____

_____

_____

_____

_____

_____

Chapter 19

HEALED

Isaiah 53:5 But he was pierced for our rebellion, crushed for our sins. He was beaten so we could be whole, He was whipped so we could be healed.

Do you believe that you can be healed?

AFFIRMATION: I am healed in Jesus name.

During the time that Christ walked on earth as fully man and fully God, He was exposed to ridicule, beatings, abandonment, rejection, denial, lies and any other negative thing you can imagine. Why did He do all of that? He did it so that we did not have to endure and could be forgiven. Do you recall when I mentioned about the priests making atonement for the sins of the people once a year? Well, this goes back to that.

Had God not sent his only Son, Jesus (what a sacrifice, could you have sent your son/daughter to be killed for others?) to be the ultimate sacrifice to atone for the sins of all people; I mean people in the time of past, present, and future. Where would we be today? *John 3:16 (NLT) For this is how God loved the world: He gave His one and only Son, so that everyone who believes in him will not perish but have eternal life.* Jesus made it possible for you and me to be able to confess directly to Him for our sins and seek forgiveness. He made it possible for us to be healed of all infirmities and sickness. Don't get me wrong, there are plenty of things wrong in this world, but can you imagine what it would look like otherwise?

Jesus took on all the situations that we as individuals face today. He took on our rejection, abandonment issues, trust issues, unforgiveness, lies, ridicule, comparison, hurts and pains so that we could be healed. When I say healed, I mean that you and I could seek to be reconciled to the Father and live in freedom from the issues that plague our day-to-day lives. Whatever you are dealing with, you do not have to remain in. You can be free of those toxic and negative mindsets.

I do not, nor will I ever claim to have it all together. Nor will I claim to be any better than the next person, but I can say that I am not where I once was in mindset. Since being on this journey, because that's what it is, of rediscovery and healing, the two BIGGEST things I have learned is this: 1. THERE ARE LEVELS TO THIS WHOLENESS THING! And 2. You may/may not be responsible for the things that happened to you, but you are RESPONSIBLE FOR HOW YOU HEAL!

PRAYER KICKOFF: God, thank you for sending and sacrificing your one and only son for my sins and healing. Jesus, thank you for being the ultimate sacrifice for me, without you I don't know what life would be like.

REFLECTION:_____

_____

_____

_____

_____

_____

_____

_____

_____

_____

_____

_____

_____

_____

_____

_____

_____

_____

_____

_____

_____

_____

_____

_____

_____

Chapter 20

LOVED

Jeremiah 31:3 (NLT) I have loved you, my people, with an everlasting love. With unfailing love I have I drawn you to myself.

What does it mean to be loved by God?

AFFIRMATION: GOD LOVES ME, UNCONDITIONALLY!

I saved the best one for last! The love of God, once realized, is the most powerful tool imaginable. With God's love there is nothing you cannot do, dream, accomplish, conquer, overcome, achieve, fulfill, execute and be. My friend, Suga, sweetheart, this is the type of love that gives you superpowers. If someone asks you what your superpower is, tell them "God's love!"

1 John 4:16, 18-19 God is love, and all who live in love live in God and God lives in them. And as we live in God our love grows more perfect. 18. Such love has no fear, because perfect love expels all fear. If we are afraid, it is for fear of punishment, and this shows that we have not fully experienced his perfect love. 19. We love each other because he loved us first.

Here is what God's love does:

1. Helps you to love/forgive others, even when wronged

2. Keeps no record of wrong.

3. Helps to expel fear.

4. Removes the fear that God is harsh and likes to make people suffer for their wrongdoing.

5. Gives you grace.

6. Keeps you.

7. Heals your heart.

Those are just a few examples of what the love of God can do. When I learned to accept the love of God, I no longer felt unworthy. It is pretty rough to walk through life feeling like no one loves you; or worse yet, not loving yourself as I did for 45 years.

The reasons for feeling that way varied for me. The constant comparison to others by loved ones, men telling me no one would love me like them, or love me at all, and me telling myself that I was unlovable. Situations caused my self-esteem to be extremely low, to the point of non-existence. Consequently, I accepted things, people and situations that I should not have and probably would not have, had I been aware of God's love for me and having love for myself.

Whatever the narrative that you have spoken or heard, the truth is, it is all a lie. You are loved. God loves you, and He is the most important and influential one. Once you know that, it is easier to begin to learn to love yourself. Loving yourself leads to better situations for you. Your standards now become elevated. You learn to teach others how to treat you and you will not accept any less. You begin to erect healthy boundaries that you will not allow others to cross. Yes, someone is bound to test you, but stand strong and firm on your position; they will either rise to the occasion or move on. If they move on, they were not for you in the first place. You have to be willing to accept that they cannot handle your truth or assertions.

When dealing with family, this is where you will be tested the absolute most. Just a warning. They are used to who you were and will try to define you as conceited, different and any other negative connotation they can attach to you. Know that people are comfortable with the you they can manipulate. People are selfish by nature, so if they cannot get something from you to suit their needs, as was customary, they will rebel against you. Think it not strange if it occurs. Your job is to love them despite their reaction. Remain consistent in your new identity and attitude and they will eventually come around. Again, the key is consistency, they need to see that you are not just "putting on" or "getting new."

Finally, the love of God shown through you to others has a potent possibility. Meaning, the love you show someone has the potential to draw them out of a negative situation. For instance, let's say you come across someone that has contemplated suicide because they feel no one cares or loves them, unbeknownst to you. He/she may be sitting crying and you don't know why. You may encounter this person and strike up a conversation, just showing genuine concern about their welfare and reason for crying. I mean genuine, not being nosey. Let's say you are told the reason for their emotional state and you begin to assess the situation from the negative to the positive and show love and concern. Do you not know that it is possible that the few minutes you displayed genuine concern could have saved their life? All because you cared and allowed them to see a seemingly hopeless situation from a positive perspective.

You never know the impact your transformation can have on another person, in addition to the impact on self.

PRAYER KICKOFF: Jesus allow me to feel and display your love. Thank you for loving me when I didn't love myself. Thank you for loving me when it felt like no one else loved me. Thank you for never leaving me nor forsaking me even when it felt like I was alone. Shine your loving light into the darkest places of my heart, so that your love may soften the hard and dark places. Father replace my heart of stone for a heart of flesh that I may love you, others and myself better.

REFLECTION: _____

_____

_____

_____

_____

_____

_____

_____

_____

_____

_____

_____

_____

_____

_____

_____

_____

_____

_____

_____

_____

_____

_____

_____

Chapter 21

Letters of Reflection

Dear Young Tenishia,

I am writing to you just before our 47th birthday. It has been a long journey. You have endured some really harsh circumstances, whether by your own hand or at the hand of others. You will survive. I know that you never considered suicide, but always wished there was a way to change things. I am proud of you for not succumbing to the pressures of the world and not turning to other devices to overcome and cope. For that I am extremely proud!

I want to confess to you that I never thought we would make it this far. I never thought that there was a way out or a way to overcome. I forgive you and ask that you forgive me for all the things we went through. So, in this moment, I tell you that you will learn to forgive and move on. Constantly holding on to situations was never the answer. There is no condemnation for that, I understand that you were only protecting yourself the best way you knew how. Thank you for trying and doing your best. Rest comfortably in knowing that your experiences were not just for you, they were to help a people that I have yet to see and speak to. To show them the possibilities and outcome.

I now release you from all the situations that held you back from progressing and maturing emotionally and socially. You held strong, but now it is time to allow God to be your strong tower, ever-present help and defender. I bless you now to move into your purpose and calling. From my current vantage point, the sky is the limit to what you will achieve.

I Love you

The reconciled, mature and healing Tenishia.

Dear Mom and Dad,

I write this letter with heart felt apologies for all the things, situations and circumstances that I blamed you for. I know now, as I too am a parent operating from a healed mindset, that you both did the best that you could at the time. I know that there was nothing you did intentionally to cause me harm.

I realize that looking back on situations from a parental perspective that there are always things we wish that we could change or have done differently. I am positive that this is the same for the both of you. It is my prayer that you receive this public apology as you have received the private one.

I want to thank you Mom for being there for me when I did not think things would be any better than they were and when I could not see past my pain. Thank you for being the voice of reason and positivity. Thank you for praying for me. I know that you think that I saw you as the "bad guy" growing up but know that I understand you raised me how you saw best. If I say so myself, I didn't turn out too bad. Congratulations and I love you.

Dad, despite the times and circumstances of past, I want you to know that I appreciate the effort and turn of events that have changed things. I thank God for restoration — what is understood does not need to be explained. Thanks for being my cheerleader "biased" as you say, but still. I love you too.

God, I want to thank you for the vessels in which you choose to give me life and bring me forth. They may not have known that they were the ordained conduits for the greatness that you have placed inside of me, but I am grateful. Now bless them to realize the greatness you have placed inside of them. Allow them to be used for your Glory Father, allow their lights to shine so that men may see and be drawn to you, in Jesus name Amen.

Love you,

Your Ms. Bren & Your Baby Girl

Dear Son(s),

I am grateful that God choose me to be your mother. I did not know how I could do it, but I am glad that I did. It was/is a joy to have raised you.

To my baby in Heaven, I loved you, but God knew best. Your time, although short, had purpose, but your heavenly purpose had more meaning. Thank you.

Son, although I may not have made the best decisions at times, I did the best that I could with the information I had. I am positive that in a few years you too will reflect and see what I mean. I want to apologize for raising you from my posture of brokenness. Unfortunately, I know that has had its affects, but I now try to correct or guide/lead you from a place of wholeness. We had good times, and I pray that they outweighed the bad. As long as you know that you are/were loved is all that matters to me.

Overall, I can say that, despite the circumstances, you were an easy child to raise. You had your moments, as most teenagers do, but you did not give me any major problems. That in and of itself is a testimony that not all parents can give. Thank you, Lord.

My prayer for you is to soon realize the greatness that God has placed on the inside of you and for you to be the man of God that He has called you to be. I pray that the problem on earth you were born to solve is realized and you begin to operate in that calling. I pray that you be the best father that you can be, as you are, and greater. Raise him to be even better than you are, as we as parents wish better for our children. I say greatness manifest, manifest, manifest!

To my grandbaby, I know that God has gifted you to me, and I am grateful for your presence. You bring a new level of joy and love to my heart. I could never have imagined the change you would bring until you came into this world — the unconditional love astounds me every day. Lord I promise to do my best to steward the gift you have placed on and in this baby. Gigi loves you to infinity.

I love you "To infinity and beyond,"

Mom

Take time to really listen to your heart regarding who and what to write. This exercise will add another level of healing for you. You do not have to share the letters with the person in which it is addressed to. This just allows you to release the negative feeling

Chapter 22

Sweet Baby

(This poem came to me in a dream but is directly the voice of God)

I was never really comfortable or free to just share,

All of the things my heart couldn't bear.

Once in a while my light would shine through so

I could come by to say I love you.

But often times you just weren't there so I could show

you I care. Many times, I would just linger your absence I could not bear.

Heart to Heart I so long to be, close to you my beloved baby.

I'll cradle you close until you feel me.

Safe in my love that is where you will be forever and ever until eternity.

Please understand that's been my will and plan.

This is not your earthly father but your Heavenly Father, understand.

My gift of love I command to sweep you like a flood until you land safely in my hands. You're my sweet baby.

HEART OF THE MATTER

I want to thank you for going on this journey with me. I sincerely pray that this has blessed you immeasurably. I want you to know that God loves you, that you are beautiful, talented, purposeful, worthy, lovable, kind, smart, friendly and beloved. The potential for you to heal from any brokenness is only limited by you. Take the limits off yourself. You can achieve anything that you set your mind to and that God called/purposed you for.

I want to dispel the myth that you are weak if you seek counseling or healing. That is a lie from the pits of HELL. In fact, it is when you show weakness, that you are your strongest. It takes one very strong person to admit that they need help in any situation. Find a couch to lay or sit on. Check the reference section to see the ministries that I attended, as they are nation-wide.

So, I admonish you to not stop here. There are levels of wholeness and healing to be achieved, like I mentioned before. This is a never-ending journey. If at any point you feel that you have capped out on your healing, check your pulse, because you probably woke up dead. (smile) There will always be people and situations to try you and test your healing. Rest assured, there will be times when you fail, but that doesn't make you a failure, you just didn't respond well. Give yourself grace and do better next time.

Finally, do not allow anyone to define you. Your identity is rooted and grounded in Christ Jesus. Do not dummy down who God called you to be just to suit the taste and comfortability of others. Be you authentically, unapologetically, and unequivocally!

I love you with the love of the Lord.

BIBLIOGRAPHY

"ANWA-Atl." All Nations Worship Assembly. Accessed June 12, 2019. https://allnationsatl.org/.

"Dictionary by Merriam-Webster: America's Most-trusted Online Dictionary." Merriam-Webster. Accessed June 12, 2019. https://www.merriam-webster.com/.

"Jamal Miller." Facebook. Accessed June 12, 2019. https://www.facebook.com/jamal.miller.

Johnson, Lorie. "The Deadly Consequences of Unforgiveness." CBN News. June 22, 2015. Accessed June12,2019. http://www1.cbn.com/cbnnews/healthscience/2015/June/The-Deadly-Consequences-of-Unforgiveness.

"Programs | Desert Stream." Desert Stream / Living Waters Ministries-. Accessed June 12, 2019. https://desertstream.org/programs/.

"The One University." Login. Accessed June 12, 2019. https://theoneuniversity.com/login/

ABOUT THE AUTHOR

Tenishia B. Lester is a Certified Destiny Life Coach/Mentor for individuals that need assistance in finding their purpose in life. She is currently pursuing a degree in Psychology because her goal is to become licensed in Marriage and Family Counseling. She was born and raised in New Jersey but currently resides in Georgia. She is currently a Small Group Leader at All Nations Worship Assembly of Atlanta where she also volunteers on Serve Teams for the Ministry. She has served in other leadership positions within and outside of the church, throughout the years. Family is very important to her; she has a son (another who preceded her in death) and one grandson.

Tenishia is known for her caring ways, listening ear and wisdom; characteristics that many seek her out to help them to make major decisions in their own lives. Steering others clear of the mistakes that she has made in her very own life is one of her passions. She finds joy in helping and encouraging others — she wants to see them win. As a result of experiencing years of sexual abuse, failed relationships, low self-esteem and not being secure in her own identity, she made up her mind to change the trajectory of her life. Enrolling in counseling and other healing ministries, has helped her realize that her struggles were not for her, but for the uplifting of others going through what she had experienced in her life. Writing this book was also another way for her to give hope to those wanting to give up, and tools to overcome adversity

She says "Healing....it's a whole journey."

CONTACT THE AUTHOR

Subscribe to my blog on www.tenishiablester.com

Please follow me on:

Facebook: http://www.facebook.com/tenishiablesterceo

Instagram: http://www.instagram.com/tenishiablesterceo

ISBN: 978-0-578-52982-0

Made in the USA
Monee, IL
27 May 2023

34771190R00070